There is nothing more human than death. Yet it continues to be a mystery of emotions, meanings and what to say or do in the face of it. The living have learned to share the stories of their loved ones. Ann Curran in her latest book of poetry, *The Book of the Dead*, captures the anecdotes of her family and depictions of the dead in a way that is poignant, humorous and provocative. She invites us not only into her family, but also our own families and their stories of the dead. Some of them are even true. All. emotionally so. They speak of the feelings of those who have suffered the loss. Frankly, I love Ann Curran's poems.

--Rev. Michael J. Stumpf, pastor, St Mary of the Mount, Pittsburgh, Pa.

My Book of the Dead is powerful testimony that poetry can indeed raise the dead, body and spirit, so that their presence is felt among us once again. In these beautiful, arresting, sometimes acerbic, sometimes startlingly funny poems, Ann Curran chronicles in her distinctive voice the lives of the parents, siblings, cousins, aunts, uncles and friends who once dwelt with her upon the earth. There are stories in every poem of the poignancy, joys, absurdities and tragedies that make up our oh-so-brief lives and that inspire us to conjure our own beloved dead to join the throng to whom Curran has introduced us.

--Mary Farrell Bednarowski, Professor Emerita of Religious Studies, United Theological Seminary of the Twin Cities.

This is some of Ann Curran's best work, so far (I feel I can say this with some authority, as I have published three of her books). The section entitled *Grandmas, Santa Clauses, Einstein, A-Bombs, Dirty Desks*, in spite of how irreverent it sounds, is filled with a plethora of insightful poems. They'll knock your socks off!

--RD Armstrong, publisher and philanthropist

My Book of the Dead

*Hey, they're gone, but our
memories of them are alive and well!*

Poems by Ann Curran

©2020 by Ann Curran

ISBN 978-0-9997784-7-0

First edition

Lummox Press
PO Box 5301
San Pedro, CA 90733
www.lummoxpress.com

Printed in the United States of America

CONTENTS

IV. Grandmas, Santa Clauses, Einstein, A-Bombs, Dirty Desks 72

My Book of the Dead

Ann Curran

They lived and laughed and loved and left.
—James Joyce, *Finnegans Wake*

My Book of the Dead is dedicated to all my
relatives who bear the surnames of Curran,
Curraidhin, Lydon, Scanlan, Scanlon, Cox,
Hammer, Dwyer, Gallagher, Wintermantel,
Codori and all the others. You know who
you are. With special mention of husband
Edward D. Wintermantel Jr., daughter Cristin
Curran Wintermantel, son-in-law Chris Buckley,
and sister Mary Pat "Mur" Curran

Aine ni Curraidhin

Yeah, It's All True

Lying in bed, I watch the wind
tease the ginkgo leaves so gently
it occurs to me from nowhere:
Aunt Eleanor wasn't the sole
good liar in the family.
Her stories leapt over the facts,
always pushed the humor deeper.
Jimmie could ooze such innocence
with untruths, even God believed.
That made the Holy Spirit howl
halfway across the universe.
I plead guilty to any fib
that will enhance the "Currant" tale.
So enjoy. Please forget the facts.
Some truths hide behind all our lies.

BOOK I.

My Expanded and Explosive Nuclear Family

Passing the Torch

The Unspoken

Knocky

Proper Funeral Behavior

Raid on the Pantry

In memory of Anna Elizabeth Scanlon Curran 1907-1975

It starts quietly enough:
my mother looking for a pot
and lid in the pantry cupboard.
Pots, lids, roasters, and old toasters,
cookie sheets, pie pans, three fry pans
jam shelves, slither sideways and bump.
Then the pots bang, clang, echo.
Lids slide out on the floor, slip, roll away,
clatter, bash, crash.
Sound escalates with her anger
as she whacks, smacks
misfit pots and lids together.
We kids almost laugh ourselves sick
silently in the kitchen,
bent over as decibels rise,
as she seeks the elusive lid,
the matching lid to *any* pot.
I still convulse just thinking
of it—alone, ironing,
or kneeling in church—
swallowing a huge touch of mirth,
my cheeks suddenly feeling wet
seeing so late: better
turn worse.
The cancers, the kids, the
Latin scholar
stumped with singular sad endings.
It wasn't funny at all.
But it still makes me laugh and cry.

Getting to the Bottom of Frick Park

For Daddy 1896-1964

Down in the hollow, we cook
hot dogs on shaven wood sticks,
eat them crushed with darkness,
tasting of wet ground, fresh leaves.

You toss our chocolate bars
in the tall garbage barrel,
afraid of whitened edges.
The Irish dance a football

across the grass; we'd climbed down
beyond the sound of the street,
deeper than town, to a place
I have never again found.

Gram's Taffy Pull

For Margaret Colette Scanlan Scanlon 1879-1965

The old woman throws golden strands
into the summer air. Grandkids
crowd her back porch, beg for a turn.
Never happier, she laughs out loud

as they lick their sticky fingers.
The warmth cools. The taffy hardens.
She curls inside herself again:
a distant, sad and lonely place.

Passing the Torch

Thank God, I gave
your mother that book,
said Gram, *or there'd*
be twelve of you
instead of six.

*

Sex is more important
to men than to women,
my mother says
as I, too, set off for
a May honeymoon
at Niagara Falls.

*

My father took
my mother on one date
that I remember.
"Fanny," a light opera
under the stars
at Pitt Stadium.
She giggled about it
for days like a girl.

The Goodbye Visit

When Mother calls me home to say goodbye
to Gram, busy dying in her room upstairs,

I come with my feelings buried just like
that icy, old woman's I'd grown up with.

Brass bed gone, she lies on a slim flat slab,
sides up to protect her from further falls.

I remember nothing of what I said
to her closed eyes and stern, unmoved face.

Light falls on her bed. I move in shadows,
try to make some quiet, polite exit.

She groans as though she has lost something
I turn, ask, *Are you OK?* No reply.

The Unspoken

In honor of Thomas J. Curran 1894-1964

Married at thirty-nine,
my father was always old.
It may have taken him that long
to believe in love again,
to believe in hope again.

At twenty he sailed to France
for the first horrible war
of the twentieth century.
Assigned to a medical
unit, he never uttered

a single word about
his war experiences.
During Hollywood battles,
he would dart from his seat
and never return again.

Consumer Reports ®: How to Clean Practically Anything

That dirty little mouse eats jam off my hand
as I slip around the world on the Internet.
Poor man-made hickey: no cleaning lady.
Full to overflowing with black, gunky crap.

Remove that bugger's ball.
Clean the rollers with toothpick
and cotton damp with oil.
Shine the mouse ball with cotton, too.

Now, I clean the how-to book, page 66,
that picked up a big drop
of cinnamon-stained oatmeal
from my splattered pink robe.

My last pink robe caught fire
as I backed up to keep warm
at the stove. My mother's mouth,
open, but too shocked to speak, alerted me.

This book cleans, wipes away, removes
everything but dark memories
like Daddy
     falling

                down
                        those
                                long,
                                        hard,
                                                steep,
                                                        bare
                                                                stairs
        at 810 South Negley.

Not sure if it was wine, old age or both.
Annie, he said, like an apology.
He didn't break anything. Except my heart:
slow to love, slower to forgive.

Death Watch

My father died alone
late at night
at the Veterans Hospital.
God knows he paid
his way with bombs
bursting for fifty years

in his head. Pictures
of the damaged and dead
that stunned a kid
in the medical corps.
Struck down by a stroke,
he said nothing.

If I took his hand
he would squeeze.
Just muscle reflexes,
a doctor explains.
None of his sons
or my sister were there.

Don't know why.
I followed my mother
down the hallway
where she went
for a smoke.
When we came back,
he was gone.

Send in the Leeches

They cut off her breast, removed
the diseased cradle of life
but not the tumor-feeding
ovaries. Still the cancer
stole behind their defenses
attacking distant organs
in that war-weary body.
Cobalt chewed her arm raw.
Chemotherapy pulled her hair
out in clumps and made her retch.
When the lungs fell, she quit
smoking for almost a month.

It was a case that questioned
the Creator's kindness.
A history of horrors
that won me an unwanted
berth among the high-risk
statistics. My doctors prod
and poke and order tests
that send technicians scurrying
behind lead barriers
like frightened rats.
Still they wait—so patiently—
to treat a terminal illness
with new and improved meds
that have the odd side effect
of sometimes halting the heart.

My Mother's Last House

stood sideways on Princeton Boulevard.
Faced a paper street dark with dense woods
across the road from a football field.
Four bedrooms: one for the oldest son,
one for the baby girl, a bright one

for the soldier boy who bought the house
and sometimes visited on war leave.
She slept alone over the kitchen.
Daddy, Gram gone. Aunt Maggie married.
Sgt. Jimmie and I huddled with her
at the tiny red table. She talked
of going home to Shadyside, McCabe's,
Sacred Heart. *I don't want to be buried
with those Currans. Move Daddy*, she said.
Oh, yuck, I thought. He'll drip on the grass.

Not sure why she told the middle kids,
but Jimmy and I followed orders.
He couldn't look at her casket.
The older brothers dragged him in—
shaking with sobs.

Leaving Calvary Cemetery

my sister and I run into
my childhood friend Diane Yeagley

who asks us, *How is your mother?*
We pause. Censor several replies.

No trouble breathing anymore.
After cancer attacked her breast,

vagina, lungs, it laid claim
to her entire body, on fire

as she fought for her life again.
Funny you should ask. We just brought

her a few sorry petunias.
Press Teamsters on strike again.

Nowhere to print the sweet obit
she deserved. No words to write it.

Knocky

For Margaret Scanlon Shierson 1905-1987

We called her "Knocky" for the sound
her high heels made on the wood steps
to her third-floor bedroom. Besides
we couldn't get our mouths around
Margaret. She managed an office,
which means she got others to do
the work. She carried that skill home.
I cleaned her room for a quarter.
When I helped with Sunday dishes,
she rewarded me with movies.
She got me a newspaper job
from an old editor who liked
her smile, her style, her soft-blue eyes.
She knew how to deal and with whom.
Seven priests offered her funeral Mass.

The Matriarch

When Aunt Maggie died
she left us minks, Persian lambs,
Waterford still wearing its green label,
Limoges dishes she never used,
sterling enough to support
a third-world uprising,
forty-seven different china teacups,
Miss Manners' book with a red leather
marker at "Insults from Others,"
medals and first-class relics
of assorted saints,
diamond rings, antique pins,
dozens of white gloves, cotton and kid,
Irish lace tablecloths,
a Wheeling gold coffee set
as garish as Versailles,
chipped crystal, a closet full
of clothes, all stained
where her bosom caught
the falling jam, dripping tea.
And … five years' worth
of unpaid back taxes.

When I Was Ten

For Aunt Eleanor Scanlon Keevican 1917-1973,
and Uncle Leo A. Keevican 1903-1990

Aunt Eleanor told me to marry a rich man
as she slipped her bed sheets, husband's dress shirts, curtains
through the mangle in her tiny two-bedroom house.
I thought her husband *was* a rich man but maybe
not then. *It's easy to love a rich man*, she said.
Just as easy as it is to love a poor man.
She taught me how to play Solitaire—*just in case.*

In time, her houses grew in size until she found
herself in a hotel in Brazil where she bought
amethysts to send home, delighted in
carnival as folks threw water-filled balloons
at each other. He kept the books for the steel works,
then took her home with deadly cancer. She loved him,
I guess. He never recovered from her quick death.

Little Brother

For John Curran, 1940-1993

Jack stood on his head longer than anyone.
His great "Pieface" too red. That mean nickname,
a gift from his oldest, nastiest brothers.
He must have felt lost in that big family.
How scary with four older kids, mother
busy with a new baby, dinner for ten,
laundry forever. Daddy still at work.

Jack spelled as though the alphabet itself
was some foreign tongue. But he could beat all
of us at chess. Once he bought an old car
for a dollar. Repaired it to running.
Like my brothers, I dismissed him as a kid.
Three years separated us. When he marched
off to the Army, they put him in charge
of all recruits because he was six-foot-five.
He tried to be cool. No smile. He would grunt
a reply. No words. But it was easy
to make him burst out laughing like crazy.
He struggled to learn how schools picked players
for football teams, trying to guide his son
to a scholarship. A strange world for him.

His heart stopped at Gold's Gym, a breath beyond
fifty. Three doctors dropped their weights, tried to
breathe life back into his body. The hospital
wanted his organs. No, his daughter said.

It broke his heart when he passed along
his brother's cleft palate to his first grandchild.
I wish I'd soothed his pain and yet I wish
I'd beat him at chess in at least one game.

Proper Funeral Behavior

For Josephine Vorsams Curran 1929-1994

When I went to my sister-in-law's funeral,
I forgot my PJs, undies and toothbrush.

I bought those and flowers quickly enough,
but I forgot to leave my sense of humor at home.

So, as we all sat solemn and sad at the wake
I whispered something—can't remember what—

cracked up my brother Jimmie. Her friends looked shocked
to hear his laugh. But we both felt better after that.

I Wish We Could Chuckle Again

In memory of James Leo Curran 1936-2001

I only have to see the name
Alexandria, Virginia, to open
the door to the loss of my brother.
Years of silence and no laughs from
a Republican who had tried
to convince me that Gore would lose.
That's the way the Supremes do things.
He loved political intrigue.
He loved ritual at the Tomb
of the Unknown but couldn't face
the wall of dead Vietnam vets.
Thanks to DNA, all now known.
He sorted bodies, belongings--
so little to send to families.
He lived our father's war horrors.

The Tin Lady on PBS

For Aunt Genevieve Scanlon
Ventrone 1915-2004

Sometimes when I laugh out loud
I hear my crazy Aunt Gen.
She won her fifteen minutes
of fame as The Tin Lady
showing viewers how to paint
19th century tinware
with early U.S. designs.
When she tired of spice holders,
measuring cups, wedding trays,
she started stenciling walls
even into her eighties.
None of this made her crazy,
of course, but her letters home
exploded with hot anger.
The most innocent remark
sent her into such a rage,
you would expect a singed page.

Don't write to her, Mother said.
She's really kind of crazy.
But I loved her spunkiness.
Divorced, remarried without
church approval, she carried
her guilt like Calvary's cross.
Her kids, Pat, Collie and Deb,
asked why she skipped Communion,
not to mention confession.
She shrieked but didn't explain.

They were teens when Gen told them
Pat was her son by Carl,
Ted was the girls' father.
All three kids were stunned silent—
at least in front of their Mom.
At 21, Pat called Carl
who refused to meet his son.
Like Gen, Pat went through divorce,
found a lovely new mate,
remade every room for them.
When I told Gen Carl had died,
she and Ted remarried in church
sometime in her seventies.
On my last visit, she'd moved
into assisted living.
Bishop Someone's Place, she said,
tickled at her Catholic home.

Complained her son, her husband.
neglected her. Her daughters
lived across the continent.
When she died at 89,
Ted wed his secretary.
That lasted a mere three years.
He disinherited Pat,
the kid he had adopted.
Her son, the love of her life
who hadn't spoken to her
in years. My sympathy note
provoked a blast back from him.
She'd passed along her writing
venom to her only son.

Shoot at Arlington

When my brother Jimmie died
I quit taking pictures.
The hunt for what would stun
stopped dead in a blur
that would touch and tear.
Four falls later I returned
to Arlington's white crosses,
golden trees, too many losses.
I clung to the tripod
taking pictures of the grave
and the graves. So brave,
so cold. But the ache lives on.

Flawed

He always felt flawed
with that imperfectly
repaired cleft palate.
His taunting peers saw
and heard the difference.
He did the dirty jobs
at home. Cleaned toilets
so well neighbors
hired him to tidy theirs.
The only devout
altar boy among
the four sons,
he never snitched wine,
never mocked the priest.
Even in Vietnam
he tidied up
after the Army,
shipping bodies home,
regretting the loss
of personal items.

At forty, he listened
to his mother's advice
about marrying
a woman born with
a missing digit or so.
When his mother died
he found his matching
mate again but never
brought her home where
such flaws are first felt.

That Old Houdini Trick

In memory of David P. Curran 1935-2005

He worked in steel, in the mill, on the Mon.
In the union and out. He talked politics.
They're all grafters. Took violin lessons
at forty. Knew Beethoven inside out.
Loved any dirty story. The queen crushed
having intercourse with a heavy horse.
I gave him Twain on farts. Gingerbread men
with walnuts at the appropriate place.
Born on the Fourth of July, he believed
for years the firecrackers, fireworks
celebrated his very own birthday.
As a boy, he refused to play football
as though he knew of his missing kidney.
The Army placed him in a germ warfare
center where a recruit died of plague.
He read history—two books at a time.
First in the food line, he shared our father's
taste for drink and tendency to vanish
before your eyes. Something was said. His eyes
clouded. He was gone though he had not budged.
Like our father, he moved his brood into
a widow's house and raised four gifted kids
who saw more Civil War sites than enough.
Like our grandfather, he gambled and lost.
Like our mother, who drove over a hillside
and never drove again, he gripped the wheel
as though he were on a roller coaster.
He decided when to die, after all
the tubes, infections, rehab, shifting

modern medicine and insurance could mount.
Don't talk me out of it, he said to me
a month shy of our father's final age.
The morphine drip let him go long before
he was gone—like that old Houdini trick.

Dear Oldest Brother

For Thomas J. Curran 1934-2009

Now that you're gone, I regret
ignoring you during life.
You were up there at the top.
I was just the first girl child,
but I ironed your underwear.
Yes, mother made me do it.
You pitched a ball in my face.
Still have the deep, ugly scar.
You were my wedding escort,
leading me down the long aisle
giving me so much silver
I don't use and plan to sell.
You dumped my brand-new husband
from water skis on the Mon,
driving your boat like a loon
zig-zagging up the river.

You always hung with trouble:
high school, Army, the steel mill
and the battle with David,
your first competing sibling.
All complicated with drink.
Smashed, you spoke black English.
No one could understand why.
When I favored Obama,
you told me to kill myself.
Did we come from the same womb?
Was it cozier for me?
I'm sorry I cut you out

of potlucks for family, friends,
but I did bring leftovers.
Then stopped because of your health.
And you went and died on us.
The mailman called the police.

Last Skirmish

Thomas, alone in the kitchen,
wouldn't lie down even for death.

Wouldn't stand up for it either.
No one dared mess with the first-born

except David, the second-born.
Their fight about a car or girl

or both made a skirmish of battles
Thomas fought with the U.S. Army,

the union, the company, white
and black work and drinking buddies.

David's kids were his closest friends.
He hung with them at gatherings.

They roared over Tommy stories.
They thought he was hilarious.

Mary Pat Signs The Book of the Dead

*For Father Warren Metzler 1937-2016, pastor, St. James
Church, Wilkinsburg; Thomas J. Curran 1934-2009, and Mary
Patricia Curran*

When Tommy died, Pittsburgh's kindest pastor
agreed to take him into the church he never went to,
let his guilt-ridden family mourn some more about
the failings of his life and theirs, for stepping aside

from the sorrow he evoked, the memories he echoed.
Even a cousin who had reason to hate the late

showed. We begged God for mercy on him and on us.
Tommy was the only kid who refused to speak ill

of our pained, brilliant, alcoholic father.
We made Zeke record him in *The Book of the Dead.*

Our big brother had given her that mean nickname.
Our kindest brother called her Murray or Mur.

Book II.

What They Tell Me About Heaven

Assorted comments from Heaven dwellers, including Tucker, an English-speaking Persian cat.

"God's a nice guy. We talk cars. The Holy Spirit is a riot!"

"God can get a little cross at times, but she always means well."

'Brits are so friendly, it's scary.'

'No place is perfect.'

'Meow, Meow, Meoooow! Translated from Cat:

Jesus and Mary agree I deserved better than that popcorn can you buried me in.

Brother Jimmie Curran: No one looks at me and sees a cleft palate or figures pity parties led me to this perfect place. The Boss lets me smoke when we have coffee at Café Cravings.

Brother David Curran: I don't know why my brother hates me. It doesn't matter. I don't get nervous driving here. No potholes, red lights or cops. Three is the lucky number. All betting is legal. You can't lose.

Brother Tommy Curran: There are no bars, no booze, but a feeling you've just been there. I can't find David anywhere. I miss him. I'm not sure why I went wrong or how I landed in Heaven.

Brother Jack Curran: You know every word doesn't have a vee, double u, ex, wye, or zee in it. No spelling tests. You're happy and don't ask why. God's a nice guy. We talk cars. The Holy Spirit is a riot!

Gram Margaret Scanlan Scanlon: No one is poor. You don't need china or silver to prove it. You don't have to hide your goodies. Nobody needs to steal. I'm surprised I made it. I'm lying low most of the time.

Jim Marcoly: You can roll in the grass all day, dance all night. There are no dirty words. Almost anything goes. But ask. God can get a little cross at times, but She always means well.

Great-Uncle James Scanlan: Boxing hurts and doesn't make you a good person until you give it up. I see Annie again. Thank you for coming to my bedside, recording my death. Caring.

Great-Aunt Bridget Scanlan Hayes: God knows it hasn't rained since I arrived. I'm not used to all this sunshine. Brits are so friendly, it's scary. I met your grandpa, my brother. He misses not meeting you and me.

Aunt Maggie Scanlon Shierson: I got my own house. Cozy as all get out, full of crying, laughing, plotting little kids. I love them all. It seems I've been at this Heaven thing for years, living or dead.

Aunt Gen Scanlon Ventrone: Well, no place is perfect, but I'm painting old tins again. My hands don't hurt. There were questions about my nasty letters home. I have to apologize to so many. The Big Guy insists.

Uncle Ted Ventrone1915-2008: You win every case. You can convince the best judges how this fire happened and who the hell is to blame for it. That's fun. I got in for marrying Gen in her church at 70. What affair?

Cousin Patrick Ventrone 1938-2016: Hey cousin Ann, I know you didn't like it when I moved into your baby buggy, but it was just for a short time. And I didn't pee all over you.

Collette Ventrone 1944-2014: When you grow up in Jersey and work in Texas, you can't imagine a place like this. And it changes every day in every way. I'm strong enough to mix oils. Plenty to paint.

Aunt Eleanor Scanlon Keevican: I don't know where the women's club up here meets, and I don't care. My granddaughter, Courtney Cairns Keevican arrived yesterday. She's so young and lovely.

Uncle Leo A. Keevican 1913-1990: It's like a golf course that's impossible to beat, but you conquer it every time. You never need to buy balls. Everything is free. Quite a cut above our late country club.

Pop-in-Law, Edward D. Wintermantel: You wouldn't believe the fuss over apples up here. They brought in angels to rave about my picking them at 82. Shoot, they even played a video of me up a tree in Sewickley Heights.

Mom-in Law, Grace Hammer Wintermantel: God gave Bernie a fancy trailer that floats on a cloud. I don't think he's going anywhere else for the rest of eternity.

Henry L. Hillman 1918-2017, Pittsburgh billionaire: Elsie finally got the downsizing she wanted. Now she says it's too small to celebrate Jesus's birthday properly. No problem. He's tied up with St. Teresa of Calcutta that day and never misses Cristi's Christmas tree.

Tucker, the cat who speaks English: There are no dogs here except at the zoo where they bark at the dinosaurs. They annoy God, but Mary thinks they're the cat's meow. Jesus and Mary agree I deserved better than that popcorn can you buried me in.

Mother Anna Elizabeth Scanlon Curran: There are no kitchens, no laundries, no unmade beds. No crying babies. That's enough for me. God is everywhere, Very friendly. Sometimes pretty funny. Makes me LOL.

Daddy Thomas John Curran: I got a late start at this. Moved from taking care of my mother to taking care of her mother, her sisters, our kids. Never really got it all right. Never told myself no one gets it all right. God reminds me of that almost every day.

Patricia Sullivan Dolan: Heaven is a walk on Slea Head Drive in a warm drizzle. It's the friendliest neighborhood. New people, new places, new news—like a chat out back over the fence on Monterrey. People care. Sweet Jesus is everywhere. No one wants to leave. and there's Hilary Masters from up the street. Such a kind man. Still hanging with poets, writers, editors. Still likes to cook in a dirty apron. HEY, Harry Dolan made the cut. I'm not surprised.

Stay in Touch

One Day You'll realize
you have more dead friends than
live, and you can talk to them.
Sometimes they'll answer back
in ways you can't explain

without getting locked up.
You'll finally understand
the Communion of Saints,
how they hold together
in Spirit—one times three.

Between the Barriers

Sorrow always creeps up on me.
I close the door, the windows, all
openings. But like the spiders
and bugs of winter, it slips in
between the barriers and bites
at the edges of my defense.
Happy memories only hurt.
They are no more and can't happen
again. Loss blankets all in grayness.
Even the sweet escape of sleep.

Book III.
Sometimes Tears Come as a Surprise

Last of the Immigrant Irish Servants
In memory of Sarah Curran 1897-1994

She wasn't twenty when she left Ireland
and Connemara, home of loneliness
so profound people answer the wind's call.
She joined her step-sisters at McCune's house.
They already had a servant named Sarah
so they called her Sadie. We didn't know
her job. Maybe she did the laundry.
Sixty years later she was still in shock
about the basement bathtub for the dogs
who, like her, enjoyed a pension for life.

That pension with a call-if-you-need-more
clause, helped me open the nursing home door
for her when the oil tycoon passed away.
My father's cousin, she'd come to our house
sharing gifts from the McCune family farm.
She gave me Irish cousins in Galway
and the past and place where I had begun.
She sailed home three times in seventy years.

Stone deaf, she thought planes would bother her ears.
In Ireland, they called her Auntie Sarah,
and watched her run to the thatchless cottage
first thing on every trip home to Spiddal.
She found a family with fellow servants.
The chauffeur took her to Mass each Sunday.

When she died at ninety-six she didn't
attend her own funeral—no casket,
no flowers, no friends remembering her.
She shared her memorial with a stranger.
She left me a Japanese knockoff Hummel—
a child with hands in a tub of bubbles—
looking like a young laundress in training;
enough money to buy a computer
with hard drive now called *SarahCurran 3;*
a spot or two in her century-old
plot in Calvary Cemetery; and
her well-used Connemara marble rosary.
You can feel the groove her thumb rubbed
on the heart leading to the decades.
Broken Jesus' arms end at the elbow.
She tied him to the cross with strands of string.

Sudden Grief Syndrome

Sometimes, tears come as a surprise.
The brain doesn't take part at all.
Chest heaves, gasping in too much breath.
Heart hurts, struck with loud, enraged words
from a mean man with a pig's valve in
his ticker and a fourth wife who
keeps him on a sharp, short chain.

*

At a sad Day of Remembrance
I read the names of dead children,
Nazi-gassed in the Holocaust.
Whimpering, cold with no blankets,
carried by their frightened parents
through the showers that were not wet.
I pause, can't complete the long list.

*

At cousin Sarah's funeral
at Marian Manor's chapel,
there are no old friends, some family—
a crowd of O'Malleys and me.
She held her faith tight for nine decades.

Died with frantic hand in a cross
to head and heart, left, right shoulders.
Repeat, repeat again, repeat again.

She holds her Galway rosary.
I stand to read at her last Mass
and tears appear between the lines,
wash away the words and the prayers.

My First Death

For Great Uncle James Cox Scanlan 1874-1955,
a boxer and Pittsburgh policeman. He fought 64 bouts,
55 percent knockouts. Fought for the Australian
heavyweight championship twice and lost.

Even in his eighties
he filled most doorways
and left tall men
shrinking in his shadow.

They say he knocked out
Jack Johnson with one punch
(papers called it a draw).
At our house he drank
Cambridge tea—hot water
with sugar and cream.

They say he took Grandma's rings
for safekeeping--Grandpa
was a gambler--
and never gave them back.
She sewed violets around
his greenhorn portrait.

They say he never married
the woman he loved
but kept her picture
in a trunk in the attic
and spent hours there.

He came from Kerry at two,
everyone knew, but years
later his daughter said,
no, she felt sure
it was East Liberty.

He seemed a heaving mound
when he lay dying
in the corner of a ward.
We kept our coats on
waiting for him to go.

My Acting Career, Part One and Two

In our Music Room—christened
by singer Aunt Maggie—I practice
piano while thunder grumbles,
lightning splashes day on dark windows.
A sharp strike explodes nearby,
cues drama for a ten-year-old.
I scream and fall dead on the floor.
The whole family comes running in
from chatting in the dining room.
When they see that I'm not struck
but shaking with restrained laughter,
they really want to kill me.

*

This is a gruesome, staged murder.
Death on the kitchen linoleum.
Little brother Jack pours Heinz ketchup
on my neck, my hand, the big knife.
It doesn't fool Mother at all.
She makes me wipe up all the blood.
No mention of kitchen killing,
a visit to the psych guy or
getting carried away with play.

Dum-de-Dum-de-Dum-de-Die

I back away from the stage,
write Dum-de-Dum-de-Dum-de-Die.

Sit beside Archie Bunker's wife
while her daughter rewrites my lines

and blood runs all over the set.
Success was hearing people laugh,

a reaction I expected
about a grim, ironic tale.

Our Step-Grandson

In memory of Christopher Buckley Jr. 1985-2015

I forgot to take my magic pills
and three days later, the body screams
a rough reminder: I am as cold
as ice-skating on Panther Hollow,
trying to keep up at 10 with Jimmie,
with a bonfire way off in the distance.
Three blankets can't stop the shaking.

The dry retching drives me to bed.
Then the worn body knows what to do.
I get it: why a longtime hooked kid
would break into his father's home,
empty the change from a piggy bank,
ignore his stepmother's jewelry, tea set.
And now I'm ready to forgive him.

This glib, first-born who once slept beneath
our Christmas tree after a long stop
in the bathroom and some silly talk.
We watch his happy childhood, recall
rehab at fourteen (nearly half his life).
March glum behind him to the altar.
It took a lifetime to learn this lesson.

My Godfather

For Joseph C. Curran, 1908-1981

My godfather was an astronomer.
Not academically, but just for fun.
I don't think his feet ever touched the ground.
He worked in numbers at classy, old Horne's.
Kept designers in check with estimates.
The rich wanted to know the cost upfront.
They expected a deal for their big buy.
Joe didn't make enough to live alone.
Spent his life with his sister's family.
He had sent Scott Green to dress our three homes:
The first as newlyweds down to downsizing.
Scott passed Joe's brief bio along to us.
Not sure I read it or where I hid it.
For shame. He's one of two Currans I knew
before going to Ireland and finding
a fun crowd of cousins who looked like us
except they weren't as tall as the Scanlons.
Nice, thoughtful relatives who came to see
us and O'Malley cousins in Da Burg.
Though I worked at Buhl Planetarium,
saw the Foucault Pendulum knocking down
circled pegs as Earth did its daily spin,
I never talked astronomy with Joe.
Growing up on Mount Washington, Joe felt
a few steps closer to planets and stars.
One glimpse of ringed Saturn stunned me for life.
I understood Joe's nighttime obsession.
The world shrinks as you skim the universe.

Good Friday 2013

In memory of brother-in-law Joseph Bernard Codori 1933-2013

It looks like a roaring fire in the woods
holding its circle, not spreading beyond.

The sky forms a flag with blue, white, peach stripes.
The forest flames shrink to a small campfire.
Then just a spark. Blue stripes swallow the peach.
Houses below the woods sink down in dusk.

This brief blaze marks Beanie's last day on Earth
and underlines the longevity lie.

They Laugh and Cry Over Coffee

For John Kleman, and the Kleman family

Their inner circle bulges with friends
whose last names are one letter long:
Bill W., Rick V., Jill G., Hank M.
More than a few O apostrophes.

Once he was the drunk. Then the rehab guy.
When he died, crowds came for coffee, stories
about how he took the crucial call.
They were grateful for their sober new lives.
The Klemans never came to our parties,
but kindly explained the danger in that.
So we met for coffee and sweets instead—
way too seldom for such fine friends.

Echoes of Singing

I've been singing in choirs most of my life.
Maybe my hearing was shouted to death.

I remember one Christmas midnight Mass
buried in a bunch of fortissimo

sopranos, my ear crackling with sharp pain
as though something was broken forever.

Love the after-sounds of choir practice.
The songs that run suddenly through my head.

A hum at first and then words from my lips.
No prompt, no thought, no cue, they come and go

like a Holy Spirit tickling my brain,
fluttering through like a quiet blessing.

Born Just in Time

For Cristin Curran Wintermantel
and her Daddy

Three siblings and a miscarriage arrived
before me, and that was just half the pack.
Each birth came with a physical problem
before today's genetic counseling
that could have reduced our family by three.
Not to mention that one of those was me.

I would have missed the butt-smacking welcome.
I would have missed the youngsters: Jack and Mur.
I would have missed growing into my life.
I would have missed people and what they make:
chateaux arching over rivers. Laughter
that pierces so deep, water runs down cheeks.

Bridges, books that carry us across the dark.
Music that gives math a glorious name.
I would have missed the miracles: giraffes,
tectonic plates, slices of moon, our hearts.
I would have missed the baby that someone
grew and entrusted to me and to you.

The Telltale Toe

*For Charles C. Stuebgen, Pittsburgh Post-Gazette
photographer 1903-1994*

When Cristi was six months old,
Stueby came out to shoot her.
Babies look great in diapers,
he says. I remove her dress,
pink pleats and small pearl buttons.
Leave her ruffled panties on.

She's a chubby, well baby.
Gorgeous lips wet with teething.
He looks at her, and her eyes—
big, green and inquisitive—
turn to Mom and the rattle.
She leans forward, fingers, toes

mix together on the right.
Left, the underlying toe
we barely noticed.
Years later a doctor asks,
*Which one of you has a toe
like that?* We admit: *Neither.*

On the Good Ship Lollipop

My daughter and I sail summer away
on the muddy Monongahela
looking green and clean in July sunshine.

Kids chatter, point at bridges above,
small craft backing into the water.
Then a sudden silence fills the air.

Police on shore snag a floating body.
I turn, hold a hand over Cristi's eyes.
We still recall that decades-old scene.

A Fish Story and Dinner at McCormick & Schmick's

While we sleep, Armageddon strikes our fish.
The side wall of their wet world cracks open
like a California earthquake. It spills
to the floor, through the floor, waters the buds
of pink flowers on the dining room wall,

creeps across our daughter's bedroom floor,
finds the fastest route to the chandelier
below. *Save the fish*! our kid shouts in tears.
They squirm in the last drops of life. We dump
them in a bucket of spigot water.

Rush them off to the mercy-on-pets place.
The insurance guy swallows his laughter,
doesn't bother to come take a look.
We love our new wallpaper, don't replace
the fish jail. Try luscious trout dressed in nuts.

My Last Lamb Chops

In Ireland people paint sheep.
A splash of red on O'Malley's.
Blue to ID the Buckley herd.
These future sweaters and chops
don't always follow the leader,
wander off, look for greener grass.

Maybe Yankee sheep get marked, too.
An urban dweller, I don't see
lamb till farmers' markets bring them
dressed for grill or the oven.

No more mournful baas from lambs or sheep.
We've become vegetarians.
The first time I broiled lamb chops,
the little buggers caught on fire!

I call to my man up a tree
in the backyard. No quick response
till I shout, *The chops are on fire!*
He and saw drop to the ground.

A handful of salt kills the flames
and cremates those chops to dark dust.
I remember my last lamb chops
standing on a LeMont platter,
baffled about how they got there
when they were just looking for lunch.

Dolan's Irish Home

For Pat and Harry Dolan

How they loved it. Their kids still do.
The neighbors smiled on the change, too.
Last owner moved his mother out,
gave her a house with heat hotter
than two fat hunks of sun-dried turf,
warming your front while your back freezes.

Up the hill from the fierce Atlantic.
The old house reserved for their guests.
Winds rattle the windows, shake floors.
Even the Dolans turned their backs,
stayed at Molly's guest house while workers
turned the attached barn into
a charming one-floor apartment.
A big window looks out to the sea
in the living-slash dining room.

I visited for years, didn't know
their shower had its own heater.
Yes, no heat in the old bathroom.
Guests slept in robes and blankets.
They tried to ignore poison plates
for night-visiting mice or rats.
The price was right. The hosts charming.

To Keep Her Safe

they lock the door.
Never explain

the strange cell phone.
So when a cloth
burns, she throws it
to the wood floor,

stamps it once, twice.
Her knees warm, hurt

as the fire grows.

Her son, next door,
hears the glass crack.

Mom burns to death
behind the door.

They blame themselves.

After a Certain Age

my darling daughter rules,
your back should be covered.
No kiddo, that's not right.
After a certain age
you ain't got anything
that will earn approval.
My black hair has turned white.
My skin is now so thin
all veins are visible.
Bits of blood may escape.
Breasts fall for gravity.
All skin slithers downward.
We all have arthritis.
I have a close cousin
of rheumatoid—maybe.
No blood confirmation.
Can't say joints are collapsing.
Here, take this. Blood tests tell
if it is killing my kidneys.
My six-thousand-dollar
hearing aids don't work well.
I drive without glasses
but need them to read.
Carpal tunnel flings rackets
across the tennis court.
I can't shuffle the cards.
I never could do that.
Maybe I should become
Muslim. Hide the grim truth:
Bodies die by degrees.

She Blazed at Close of Day

For Aunt Emma Brush Hammer 1913-2004,
and her fun hubby, Uncle Andy 1908-1991

Emmie had a heart wide open
to the world. When dementia struck,
street people became her best friends.
When they needed *milk for the kids,*
bread for dinner, she emptied her purse.

When she drove to new neighborhoods
just to see what they were like,
she couldn't find her way home again.
When she went to her husband's church,
which she had refused to join for years,
and took Communion, then they knew:
something was terribly wrong.

When she led an escape attempt
from the secure wing of the home
with six of her closest buddies,
her daughter understood at last
how parents fall in love with kids
broken in all sorts of ways.

His Last Blanket

For Dennis A. Molyneaux 1933-2010,
who's probably wreaking havoc in Heaven.

He was the sixth child in the family.
His wife begged him not to jump
from the balcony into the pool,
setting a bad example for the kids.
He jumped and jumped and jumped again.
Some of the kids mimicked his madness.

He ran wild into life gobbling
all it could offer and then some.
A few drew the line when he spoke
in tongues at the local monastery.
Upbeat beyond belief, he swept
his sensible wife, a dance instructor,
off her feet on the ballroom floor.
He became a social worker. Brought
unbridled joy into dark corners. Perhaps
he wrapped his sorrows in humor.

When he had his stomach stapled,
the family snuck a pizza *with everything*
into the hospital. That operation
began decades of health problems.
They never changed his outlook.
The child of immigrants, he loved
the land they left behind. Visited
Ventry, Ireland, for a month at a time.

Dialysis three times a week
did him in. *It's no way to live*, he declared.
They laid him out in an Irish blazer,
Pitt necktie, rosary in hand,
Claddagh ring circling his finger.
Bells of Ireland stood silent.
A tiny gold angel with sparkling
green shamrock lights on his last blanket.
Sure, he looks like he fell asleep,
dreaming a gag he wants to wake
and share with the gang of his friends.

When They Go Before They're Gone

For my best friends: Mary Mackin and Pat Dolan

With the sun scaring me indoors
and the heat dittoing that choice
I went to visit two old friends.
Pat remembered that she forgot
plans for lunch with another friend
till Judy came to collect her
from her assisted living home
after she'd already had lunch.
Just as well. Her wheelchair weighs
more than an old lady should lift.
She made the fatal choice, choosing
her wheels over a walker
just because she felt safer there.
She forgot: use it or lose it.

Mary made no choices at home
with a caretaker who censored
family news, whispered about her
in her presence. Blaming new drugs
for her confusion. Mary asked
three times, *How is your little girl?*
I gave her three different answers
about my forty-year-old daughter.
In case she noticed a repeat.
In the past I went to her house
for laughs. She always had a joke
or two ready to tickle you.
Today she didn't laugh a lot.
She smiled in air-conditioned cool.

Final Touch

For Aunt Elsie Wintermantel 1912-2012,
and Uncle Harry Wintermantel 1907-1991

The night before Harry died,
Elsie hugged him and held him.

And that was a great comfort
to her. Perhaps to him, too.

When she awoke, he was gone.
Cold, silent, beyond her warmth.

First Next-Door Neighbors

For Jockey, Missy and Vivian

In the cellar the old man
stares into the open furnace
telling tales of floors
beneath the flames.

In the attic, the spinster
weeps about hillsides,
forests and fields
ravaged for an interstate.

In the garage, the old man
sobs his confusion.
*It's a common sort
of suicide,* the cop says.

On Bloomsday, June 16

For Pat and Harry Dolan and family

She died on Bloomsday. The Irish staggered
pub to pub confused by Joyce's story,
they denied his view of *snotgreen* Ireland.

We buried her on the first day of summer.
Heat dried tears. One mourner packed a pistol.
Each heart cried *No I said no I won't No.*

Bobbie's Battle

For Marilyn "Bobbie" Bates 1939-2013,
a favorite in the Squirrel Hill Poetry Workshop

I cry for each toe you have lost
for your eye blinded by a bleed

for fingers that fell to disease
for your heart longing for life, love.

Done in by damn diabetes
testing you from childhood to death.

Did tears fill your lungs with fluid?
Did your hope of independence

drive you to the last final fix—
removing your remaining toe?

Did you achieve your lifelong dream?
Did you become like other kids?

The Rearview Truth

In the same week I took
the driver safety course,
I killed a squirrel that ran
from between two parked cars
just feet in front of me.
Of course, it *was* Squirrel Hill
where these rascal rodents
run up and down trees
tear across the terrace
retreat to Schenley Park
tightrope walk the fences
appear and disappear
like something almost seen

or maybe imagined.
I didn't brake quickly
enough, then told myself
he made it. In seconds
a sorry whop against
metal, the rearview truth
lay on Beechwood asphalt.
A curve or so later
two little kids emerge
from between two parked cars.
Yes. Lesson learned. I stop.
Mom is putting them in
the road side of the car.

My Two-Cents' Worth

Robert Frost and family lie beneath
a huge block of granite. Laurel leaves
outline the edge and his epitaph:
I had a lover's quarrel with the world.

It's behind First Congregational,
around the corner from Grandma Moses
and her schoolhouse museum where people
are dwarfed by snowy farm scenes, horses, carts,

the good old days of Grandma's make-believe
in Bennington. Try Blue Benn pancakes.
Still sticky from the maple syrup.
Tourists hike the hill, pay respects to Frost,
leave their change across his name. Dimes fill
his o's, a quarter on top of his R.
I lament small change, leave my two cents' worth.

His wife wanted her ashes in the wind
over their happy Shaftsbury farm.
The new owner had enough of the Frosts
and their followers stopping by daily,
didn't welcome home the cranky poet.

What's That You Say?

For Pop, Edward D. Wintermantel
1902-1990

Two pink hearing aids,
the shade of no one's skin

connect him with a world
he barely understood—

when all the syllables
and pitches were his.

He knew farming, horses,
his kids, their kids.

how Sewickley Heights worked.
Thick farmer fingers

smudged with earth for life,
hold an apple he grew

and picked at eighty-two.
An annoyed voice asks,

Do you hear anything?
His happy reply:

I hear the red birds sing.

Cross-Country Kindness

In memory of Skip Seifried Donnelly

God, you must be happy to have Skip there.
Sweetest, kindest adult I ever knew.
Like four-year-old Cristi trying to take
my migraine away, running tiny hands
across my forehead. Damn! It almost worked.
Skip was part of the Sigma Lamb move west.
Leaving Da Burgh for California sun.
Married an old guy looking for grandkids.
A teacher, she wept about her black students.
She couldn't figure out how to reach them.

     When the old guy died, she went skiing more.
     Our friendship shrank to quick Xmas-card notes.
     I found her question to me in last year's
     Christmas card. An art teacher wanted them—
     fronts only—for kids to make their own cards.
     Her card—a splash of sparkles. Her question:
     Do I have all your poetry books yet?

     Something made me call one day. No reply.
     Sent our best card yet: Bizarro and Santa
     at Bethlehem. *Why in God's name would we
     want his picture with you?* a pissed Mary
     shouts. Camera guy waits beside Fatso's big chair.
     We never got a reaction from Skip.
     Months later a guy calls from her condo.
     *Just thought you should know. Skip died: lung cancer.
     I bought her condo. Just found you online.*

My Obligatory Dead-Dog-on-the-Road Poem

Honest to God
he was flatter
than a pancake
more like a crepe
cherry sauce dried
mashed more than once
bent in a hoop
a cardboard caught
in the rain. Death
never looked less real.

BOOK IV.

Grandmas, Santa Clauses, Einstein, A-Bombs, Dirty Desks

On the Untimely and Recurring Demise of My Late, Great Grandmother

Grandmas die three or four times
a semester. Ask any teacher.
They sometimes all belong to one
slow-witted student whose wisdom
is never found in books. They die
on glowing fall days when summer's
fingers still tease and tickle,
when the warmth that was returns to taunt
the young and set the woods on fire.
They're buried on a winter morning
with no snow, cold biting the wet cheeks
of survivors. A day when comfort
lies late in bed, an extra quilt,
a cup of tea, no need to stir.
But often they book the spring flight.
With the first burst of forsythia
grandmothers queue up all over
the country. They all long to lie
beneath that yellow-green spring
where the children of their children
so thoughtlessly dispatch them.
And if they knew, they'd understand.

That Handsome Boy

For Tom Casilli 1937-2016

He led a solitary life,
his obit announced so sadly.

A fine, handsome actor on stage
at Central and Duquesne U.

Every girl fell in love with him.
His dark hair and eyes, his silence

without a script to speak for him.
He took our hearts away, broke them.

He led a solitary life.
Last time I saw him, he was reading

alone in a dim library
about growing apricots

in a town where no one grows them.
He led a solitary life.

The curtain never rose for him.

On the Brink

We paddle inner tubes
across Rock Bottom's depths,
Shiver in the shadows
of the cliff. Tell fake tales
of bodies bobbing up.
Brave in the blue atop
that hill, we slid over.
Feet find the one safe ledge
above the black pool.

In another country
lying on a narrow shelf
above the sea, too high
to hear foam below beat
against huge, fallen boulders
we move in reckless risk
while wind screams through sunshine.
There is no other time,
no other place, no end.

Now, even in your warmth
I watch a host go alone
to that final high cliff,
and I shrink before heights
as though being careful
could save me from the dark.

Guys Who Play Santa Claus

For Paul Kontul (1904-1970), Ed Gallagher
(1922-2004), and John J. Hammer (1920-2011)

I never saw Polly's dad do his thing,
but it happened for poor kids every year.
When her mother died, Polly called me down.
Santa was raging, weeping through the house.
What was he to do with a teenage girl?
A drug rep, always on the road.
Showing his love and loss was more than enough.
They survived the quick, unexpected death.

*

Ed came in full-blown costume Christmas Eve
when our daughter at five really believed.
We were as surprised as our little kid.
She asked about dark hair peeping from his cap.
Often recalled his later transformation
from architect into water colorist.
Made the ordinary more special.

*

Uncle Joe wore my guy's face and his height.
Not like the short Wintermantel brothers.
He was Joe at home and John on the job.
A World War II vet with bronze stars hidden
away, he kept his war service alive
heading up American Legion Posts.
Commander and chaplain of Post 161.
He volunteered everywhere: at his church
vet hospitals and Santa Claus "for free."Rode his
red sleigh all over the North Hills.

Candy! Everywhere!

You don't know about those you think you know.
It creeps out at death. Candy in pockets,
in drawers, all the purses, bedside tables,
and I never saw Aunt Maggie eat it.

Thomas with his naked-girl magazines
hidden as though his mother might find them.
And him living alone for years by now.

Jimmy with his downright dirty photos
in a pouch with a roach clip in his den.
Cupboards full of fast-food death for his heart.

And me? What have I stashed away to tell
some secret I no longer care about,
or, thank God, cannot even remember.

When Diane Meets the Pope

Her Jewish husband sets it up:
a private session with the saint.

John Paul II wears a zuccheto,
which looks like a white yarmulke.

Diane's husband wears a black one
and she, the usual dark lace.

They talk about her first husband,
the children, his death, the grandkids.

All the blessings of her long life.
Her husband answers some questions

because Diane can't stop sobbing.
The pope pats her arm and hugs her.

They all laugh at such happiness.
The pope doesn't rush them away.

Universal Health Care, Part One

Just beyond the Dark Ages
the Brits invented Bedlam
for those who blubber rubbish,
sit staring at what's not there,
attack the cook, speak in tongues,
eat bugs. The odder than most.
St. Mary of Bethlehem morphed
into Bedlam. Henry the 8th,

crazy enough to marry six
times, was smart enough to turn
Bethlehem Royal Hospital
over to London. Then they hung
patients in chains from dank walls.
The public paid a penny
to visit. They brought sticks
to prod peculiar action

from the heap of rags,
the blank eyes, wild hair,
the bewildered, shackled.
A few famous inmates lived in
this world of kindness turned to cruelty.
Edward Oxford, who popped his pistol
at the carriage of Queen Victoria.
No one in his right mind, they said,

would shoot the queen.
Daniel M'Naghten, who missed
the prime minister but killed

his secretary and lent his name
to the grounds for insanity.
And Charlie Chaplin's mother.
No wonder he could make us
laugh and cry with his humor.

Big Anthony's Third Day

Almost ninety bad years after
the un-Civil War that lives on,
I learn, reading the *Post-Gazette,*
an eight-month-pregnant black woman
was hanged upside down
from a tree, set on fire, her child
cut out, cried twice before its head
was crushed by a white man's mad boot.
That was in the 1950s.

I read *The Underground Railroad.**
Georgia before the Civil War.
Whites gather on the mansion lawn.
Some from Atlanta, Savannah,
a reporter from London.
They enjoy lunch, drinks and the show:
seeing a bad slave get punished.
All slaves are ordered to attend
and watch Big Anthony's third day
of punishment for escaping.
They'd chopped off his penis, stuffed it
in his mouth and sewed it closed.
Visitors were spared the shrieking
of a man getting burned to death.

I wonder why I never heard
this hidden history before
in social studies, religion,
ethics or at least history.
I might have understood just why,
no matter how friendly blacks are

in the office, when our group meets
as a whole, blacks sit together.
They know the hate can rise again.
They've felt it since they were toddlers.

Letter in the Library Book

Deep *in Huckleberry Finn*
lay an unopened letter.
Creamy envelope, black ink:
"To Whom It May Concern—You"
He finishes the chapter,
opens the mystery missive.
It's printed, easy reading:

I hate Huck Finn 'cause he calls
us niggers. I love him , too,
'cause 'niggers' almost sounds nice
when he says it, and he loves
and cares about Nigger Jim.
But I've never met a white
who uses nigger like Twain.
Add your thoughts. Return with the book.

On the Wall of Honor

In 1951, Carnegie Institute of Technology gave Col.
Donald L. Putt (later Lt. Gen.) its Distinguished
Achievement Award. He oversaw creation of the bomb
bay that held the A-Bombs, and guaranteed their landing
on two Japanese cities. Decades later, I interviewed him.
Killed the story. Ran Drama grad Holly Hunter instead.

I have met the Devil: neat, suave, tanned
living in a California condo where widows
knock at the door delivering cookies.
We talked two hours about how he escaped
the B-17 crash, worked other numbered
aircraft. He lived among antiques, satin seats,
oil painting of himself altered to add
his latest star. Gracious, courtly.
No question pierced his armor. I was
too dumb to ask: Do the Japanese haunt you? Do you
belong on the Wall of Honor at the National Air and Space
Museum? Was there another way to end the war? Were we
getting big-time-even for Pearl Harbor?
>   The numbers speak:
>   Hiroshima....................90,000-45,000*
>   Nagasaki......................39,000-80,000
>   Pearl Harbor attack.........................2,403
>   N. Korea Trump threat.............24 million

>   *First figure, immediate deaths; second,
>   deaths in following months.

Side Trip

You don't want to go to Dachau,
the porter said. *Watch the clock*
in St. Mary's Square. See
the wooden people walk,
mock on the half hour.

The train is no longer crowded.
Nobody else gets off
at Hitler's first camp.
We walk alone
into those too-green fields.

An artist has welded
a hundred metal skeletons
together—a slim reminder.
Inside, the photos of real people
stare in horror at our horror.

Through the showers,
that look like showers,
the ovens and out
to a rain-washed world
forever dirtied by this place.

Mama's Muumuu

As bright as a Japanese street strung
with a million neon storefront lights.
A wash of fuchsia, green, olive, white.
Touches of turquoise, mustard, purple, pink,
swirling with flowers of all sizes—
white dots to flashy red with blue centers.

Not her at all, though she chose it herself.
Maybe it caught feelings she concealed.
Feelings that hung in her closet for years.
She couldn't open a gift or card
while anyone looked on. What simmered
there? Feelings warmer than Oahu's waters?
Feelings hotter than flaming, sunburned cheeks.

That Terrible Time

The U.S. government recently released some
of the papers about investigating the murder
of President John F. Kennedy on Nov. 22, 1963.

When I'm going to sleep
or waking up early
I hear the muffled talk.
Can't make out anything.
First I thought radio
next door blasting above
a late or early shower.
Then I thought maybe not.
Maybe tinnitus
hearing sounds no one hears
except those with dying
or almost dead hearing.
I write on *Four Days*, a slim book
about JFK's death.
gift of the late *Pittsburgh Press*.
He's gone and Jackie, too.
Even baby John-John.
Daughter hides in Japan, vanishes.
His prayer card asks mercy
on the soul of this guy
whose Irish eyes wobble
between a laugh and a cry.

Never Ignore a Genius

*Three of the audience fell asleep and many fought
drowsiness as Albert Einstein detailed his theory of
relativity in a Carnegie Tech lecture hall for the
first time in English.—The Pittsburgh Press, Dec. 29, 1934*

Albert could understand all right.
Those three snoozing brutes in the front row.
Their mass was such, their energy less.
The gravitational pull tugged
at their lids, their shoulders, their heads.
By God, one even slipped to the floor.
The white-haired genius with the mournful eyes
had never liked schoolrooms himself.
Now he sputtered, radiated quantum doublespeak
telling old truths in his new tongue.
But he knew every molecule in that room
throbbed ten to the thousandth power faster
and the heat was relatively fierce.
Molecules have a tendency to agitate
to an uncommon degree near Nobel laureates.
He knew nuts and bolts would jolt
those engineers awake. But he wanted to talk
about the edge of the universe.
There seemed no space in the time he had.
Maybe he forgave them,
though five years later, he sold
a frail and ailing Roosevelt
on a little project called Manhattan.

Hot New News

It looks like the birth of the universe—
two black holes swirling around each other

like a merry-go-round gone musically mad.
Then they were one and sent waves across time

and space like that wild-haired Einstein had surmised.
We *see* them. Washington and Louisiana *hea*r them

chirping like birds in a windowless house of horrors.
God, this is scary! What in the hell have You done?

*

Two Hawaiian surfers have asked
NASA's help in hitching a ride

on the gravitational wave
swelling across the universe

making sweet tweets along the way.
Like NFL players with CTE,

they've banged their boards against their beans
often enough to really believe

this is a sensible request.
Like JFK's move to the moon.

First Ever: Science Watches a River Die

The yellow of the sun paints the hall wall.
Shit! It drives me to commit the rhyme crime.
Worry why the North Pole shifts and drifts east.
Displaced polar bears don't know where to sleep.
Islanders want them on top of the deep,
and Dunquin threatens to freeze Irish knees.

Last week, science said a river is dead.
No one has seen a river, and then none,
though dead-river scars mar the planet's sad face.
And listen here, it took ten thousand years.
They watched the water slosh away non-stop.
Science insists this is a brand-new twist.

The Slims River is slimmer than ever.
In fact, its three-meters-deep water hole
disappeared. Born from a dripping glacier
in Canada, the rapid melt was felt
so deeply it changed the Slims' direction.
It leapt into the Alsek River, swept

south ending in the Pacific's big mouth.
The science folks, no joke, walked through Slims' mud.
Hoodoos they call the wind-blown sediment.
The Slims River slipped away in a month.
The gods wept: *They took too many dumb steps.*
The Devil smiled: *I beguiled! I beguiled!*

CAUTION: RADIOACTIVE MATERIALS

I read the entire *Post-Gazette*
waiting for my guy to complete
his nuclear stress test. No treadmill,
no deadly bomb bursting on high.

I learn a seminarian
books a spring break in Florida
to rape, not children, but infants.
Not one or two but "multiple."

In Pakistan, a father beats
his daughter, shoots her in the head,
bags and dumps her in the river.

She lives. She with many sisters
murdered for loving the wrong man
and disgracing their fine families.

Wise Iowa dumps The Donald.
Then 22 states embrace him.

The North Pole slithers toward Europe.
Our small, abused planet adjusts,
tilts at a crazy new angle.
Makes radiation look harmless.

Tom Manning, First U.S. Penis Transplant

The New York Times, May 16; Associated Press, May 17, 2016

The penis story arose from the dead.
The patient lost all but a tiny stump

to cancer. He never noticed the growth.
He traded his penis for a longer life.

He was embarrassed sitting down to pee.
Hell! Plopped on a toilet seat, you can read

half the *NYTimes,* poop too, and not show
what a lousy shot you are standing up.

Like a punny, effing stand-up comic,
his doctor said (and I'm not making this up)

"He's up and about." He adds, "it's unchartered waters."
Dicken Ko heads the urology team.

The lucky patient smiles slyly from bed.
Tom Manning is more than a perfect name.

Next up, 300 servicemen, 18 to 22,
who suffered injuries from roadside bombs.

Premeditated

When her husband hanged himself
on the back porch, he knew
she would find him when she came
home from a neighbor's house.
He knew their daughter, upstairs
with a boyfriend, would rush down
at the sound of her mother's shrieks.
He knew things would change for them.

The daughter lost all her hair.
No doctor could explain that.
The wife went to Chicago.
They submerged her in water
three times a day, an effort
to wash away that image
he knew would last forever.

In Defense of Dirt

In memory of Pittsburgh Post-Gazette
writer Clara Herron 1924-2007

I belong to the dirty desk brigade.
Not so bad as my friend Clara who builds
great garbage heaps of paper, notebooks,
clippings, jars of jam, ticking clocks, gifts, mail
rising into mini-mountains. Guys hide
open cans of tuna beneath her stacks,
wait for the odor to offend the office.

I grow respectable piles of debris.
One day in lowering mode, I pitched
paper and uncovered a miracle.
A bug—not to get technical—that moved
somersault after somersault across
my desk. No legs, no tail, no antennae.
A circular see-through being, all muscle
that curved into each step with such sublime
skill. I have never seen its likes again.

Remains or Cremains?

Before you die
you must decide:

To lie and rot
or burn that thought.

You'll take less space
when you're a trace.

It costs much less.
It's not a mess.

You can't play ghost
when you are toast.

No coffin to drop.
No body to plop.

No one will place
specs on your face

praise your hairdo
but not to you

change your earrings
and other things

wrap you in lace,

kiss your dead face.

Choose to cremate
when you're "the late."

It's quite discreet.
No winding sheet.

So Entwined

For my finest choice of husband
Edward David Wintermantel Jr.

I don't know
if my heart
is beating

or your lungs
are breathing
in this dance

to the death.
Or how you
and I know

when the music
grows faint, stops,
who has died.

Unassisted Living

When the horizon tilts
and the great ship of life
dumps me in the drink,
I'll float and feel the waves
that lift me to the crest,

drop to the black trough.
I'll suck in the sky's glory
at dawn, in dark, in rain.
I'll forget about sharks
and tsunamis, applaud

the moderate ripples.
I'll dream of Noah's Ark,
hope for the Great Spirit
to lead me to dry land
and a place much more grand.

Done in by Carrot Vichyssoise

Frankly, I think I'll die in the kitchen.
No ER with a sign counting heartbeats.
No on-the-hour nurse waking me up,
squeezing info from a single finger,

giving me pills. Why? Your temp is up.
I'll pass away in my cluttered kitchen,
dicing onions through a burning blue blur,
Whacking my head with an immersion blender,

reducing Carrot Vichyssoise to broth.
Fingers stuck on HIGH, boiling soup flies in my face,
down green walls, across black counters.
I'll feel hellish flames before I get there.

I can't reach the sink, two feet away.
The blender smashes the glass closet doors.
I bleed from stabs head to foot and wonder
will rest-in-peace ever arrive for me?

Mourning by the Numbers

For Joe "Bullseye" Clark

He played pool at the senior center.
Belonged to the Men's Dart Club.
Kind of quiet, they said.
Beloved husband of the late Mary Lou.
Special friend of the late Patsy.
Father of three. Grandfather of eight.
Step-grandfather of three.
Great-grandfather of twelve.
A U.S. Army veteran of World War II.
Kept two Bronze Star medals
boxed in his underwear drawer.
Longtime member of the Teamsters
Union. His obit requests: in lieu of flowers
take a friend dancing. The funeral home
brims over with gorgeous blossoms.

My Hero

He wasn't the first to save his sweet butt
by joining the Navy, seeing the world.
It was no piece of cake. More a tough crust.

For fun, they swim in the mid-Atlantic
jumping off the side of the Tarawa
named for the bloodiest battle

of the war after the war to end wars.
An aircraft carrier, it holds three thousand
parents', wives', siblings' frightened sailor boys.

Sharpshooters scan the water and take out
sharks that circle the splashing lunatics.
In silence, they sit beside Korea

in the Yellow Sea or the Sea of Japan.
Gasp at the thought of bombs from above or
sly torpedoes sliding through the water

or their own planes dragging them off the deck.
Free breakfast, lunch, dinner and a haircut
at Denny's, Panera, Olive Garden

and the barbershop on Veterans Day—
not to mention, a GI Bill degree—
seems small compensation for their great risk.

Besides, you can't do much for the long deceased.

I Wasn't There.

I wasn't there when Daddy died
I stood with mother while she smoked.

I wasn't there when Jack left us.
His life seemed too much of a fuss

I wasn't there when Jimmie fell.
His neighbor reported the smell.

I wasn't there when David expired.
Repeated rehabs. He was tired.

I wasn't there at Tommy's last,
The mailman told the cops he'd passed.

I wasn't there when Maggie died.
She was a working woman's guide.

I wasn't there when Gram passed on.
I think she hurt from day one on.

I wasn't there when Mother died.
Left Jimmie weeping at her side.

It strikes me as a wee bit strange:
I vanish when Death is in range.

BIO

Ann Curran

Ann Curran of Pittsburgh, Pa., is the author of *Placement Test* (2005), an Editor's Choice Chapbook, and *Irish Ayes* (2017), both published by Main Street Rag of Charlotte, N. Carolina. *Irish Ayes* celebrates the 25th anniversary of Curran's recognition as a foreign-born citizen of Ireland. Lummox Press of San Pedro, CA, published Curran's *Me First* (2013) and *Knitting the Andy Warhol Bridge* (2016), both 100-plus page books of poetry. The latter received a Pushcart Prize nomination. Curran worked for the *Pittsburgh Catholic* newspaper, the *Pittsburgh Post-Gazette* and freelanced with *The Pittsburgh Press* and *Pittsburgh Magazine*. She edited *Carnegie Mellon Magazine* for two decades. Her poems have appeared in many publications. She is proudest of three poems on race issues, run by the *New York Times*. She and her husband, Edward D. Wintermantel Jr., live in Chatham Village in Pittsburgh. They have a daughter, Cristin Curran Wintermantel.

The LUMMOX Press was established in 1994.
The goal of the press is to elevate the bar for poetry,
while bringing the "word" to an international audience.

Now in it's twenty-sixth year, the editor/publisher
finds himself slowing down and though this unexpected
turn of events may hobble future projects,
he hopes to remain relevant... somehow.

For more information and to see the
staggering catalog of choices, please go to
www.lummoxpress.com

www.ingramcontent.com/pod-product-compliance
Lightning Source LLC
Chambersburg PA
CBHW071054090426
42737CB00013B/2347